WHO
WOULD WIN?®

ULTIMATE DINOSAUR RUMBLE

BY
JERRY PALLOTTA
ILLUSTRATED BY
ROB BOLSTER

Scholastic Inc.

16-DINOSAUR BRACKET

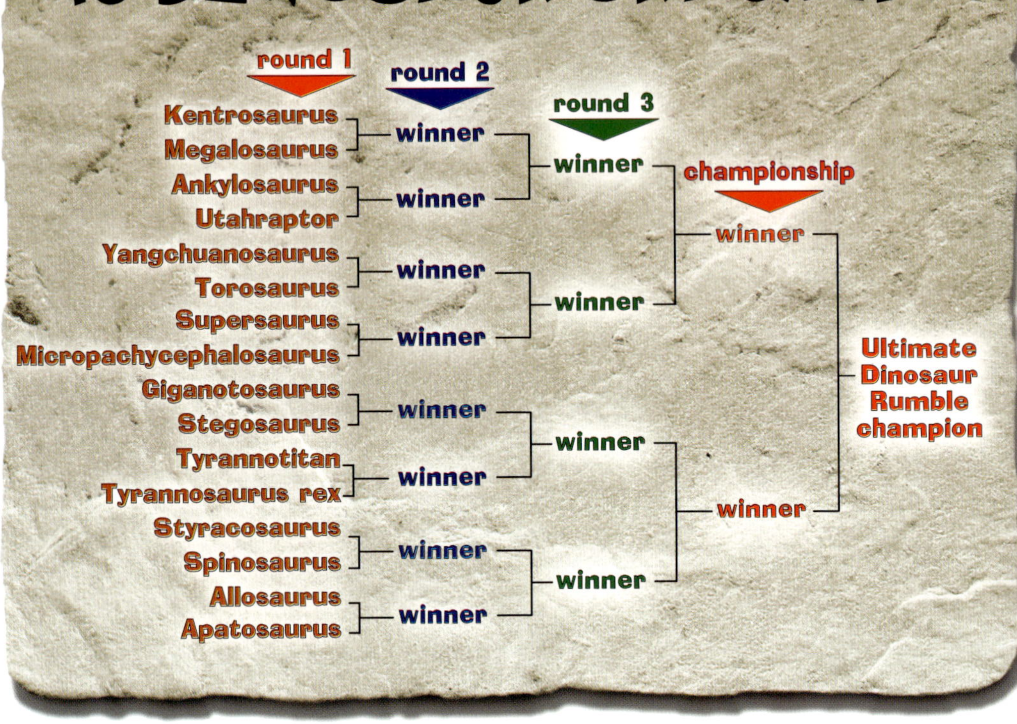

Thank you to my favorite dinosaurs: Dan, Jay, Bergie, George, Freddie, and Soupy.
—*J.P.*

Thanks to the paleontologists who pieced together these amazing creatures.
—*R.B.*

ISBN 978-93-5471-162-6

This reprint edition : September 2024
Printed in India

Sixteen dinosaurs showed up for a contest to see who is the roughest and toughest. If a dinosaur loses a fight, it is out of the contest. May the most ferocious dinosaur win!

No pterosaurs allowed!

No plesiosaurs allowed!

DID YOU KNOW?
The word dinosaur means "terrible lizard."

The first match is Kentrosaurus versus Megalosaurus. Kentrosaurus would not be easy to attack or eat. It is spiky.

ROUND 1

KENTROSAURUS VS. MEGALOSAURUS

MATCH 1

NAME FACT
Megalosaurus means "big lizard."

Megalosaurus was the first dinosaur to be discovered and named. Its fossilized bones were dug up in England.

Megalosaurus attacks with its toothy jaw but Kentrosaurus is too spiky, pointy, and bumpy.

NAME FACT
Kentrosaurus means "prickly lizard."

Megalosaurus puts up a good fight but it's out of the competition.

KENTROSAURUS WINS!

Ankylosaurus had a large, solid bump on the end of its tail. Its skin was heavily armored.

NAME FACT
The word "saurus" means lizard. Ankylosaurus means "fused lizard."

ROUND 1 ANKYLOSAURUS VS. UTAHRAPTOR MATCH 2

Utahraptor stars in the film *Jurassic World*. This movie-star dinosaur was about 23 feet long, but only eight feet tall. That is about as tall as two first graders.

FUN FACT
Utahraptor means "Utah's predator."

Is this a fair fight? Ankylosaurus is covered in armor.

Utahraptor tries to sneak up on Ankylosaurus and slice its unprotected belly. But *whoosh!* One swipe from Ankylosaurus's tail and Utahraptor is knocked silly. Ankylosaurus moves on to the second round.

ANKYLOSAURUS WINS!

DID YOU KNOW?
Paleontologists now think the Utahraptor had feathers.

Yangchuanosaurus was discovered in China. When its remains were first discovered, people thought they were real dragon bones. Some people in other places also once believed this. Yangchuanosaurus was bipedal.

DEFINITION
Bipedal means an animal that walks on two legs.

ROUND 1

YANGCHUANOSAURUS VS. TOROSAURUS

MATCH 3

Torosaurus had the largest skull of any animal that ever lived on land. Its skull was as big as an elephant.

NAME FACT
Torosaurus means "perforated lizard."

DEFINITION
Perforated means "having holes." Torosaurus had holes in its shield-like skull.

FRILL FACT
The back of Torosaurus's skull is called its frill.

After dodging Torosaurus's sharp horns, Yangchuanosaurus bites its legs and slows down Torosaurus. The limping Torosaurus is done for. In this fight, the meat-eater defeats the plant-eater. The biped beats the quadruped.

NAME FACT
This dinosaur's name means "lizard found in the town of Yangchuan."

DEFINITION
A quadruped is an animal that walks on four legs.

YANGCHAUNOSAURUS WINS!

Not fair! Who matched these two together? Supersaurus is fighting Micropachycephalosaurus. Supersaurus was a giant plant-eating sauropod.

DEFINITION
Sauropod dinosaurs had long necks, small brains, long tails, and walked on four thick legs.

ROUND 1

MATCH 4

SUPERSAURUS VS. MICROPACHYCEPHALOSAURUS

Micropachycephalosaurus is one of the longest names of any dinosaur. It's a long name, but it was a tiny dinosaur. It was only as big as a goose. Its name means "small, thick-headed lizard."

HEAD FACT
No one knows why the Micropachycephalosaurus had such a thick skull.

Supersaurus steps on Micropachycephalosaurus.
Uh-oh! Squished!

SUPERSAURUS WINS!

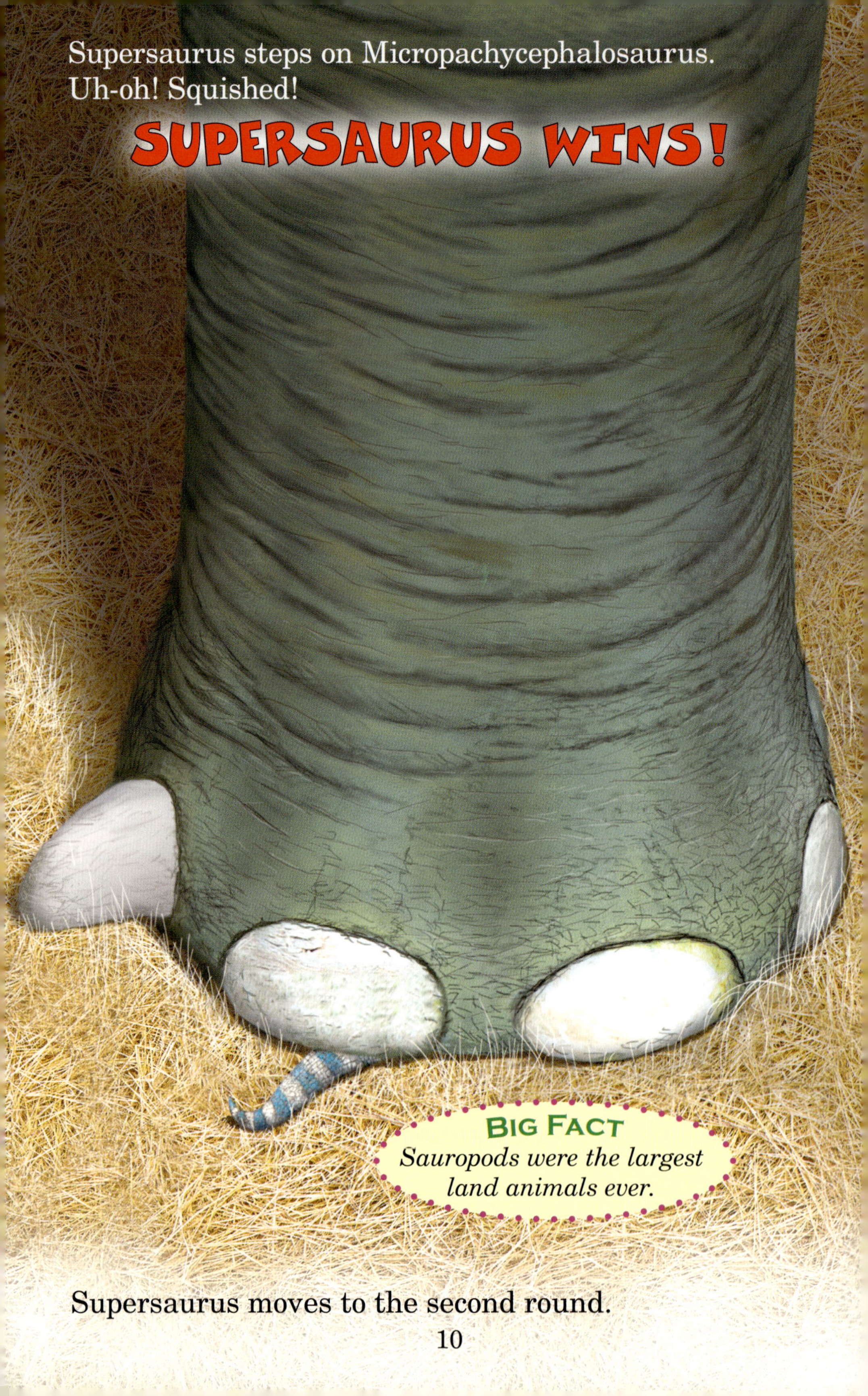

BIG FACT
Sauropods were the largest land animals ever.

Supersaurus moves to the second round.

Giganotosaurus had a huge jaw full of sharp teeth. Its jaw was six feet long. Giganotosaurus is considered the largest meat-eating dinosaur. You would not want to fight it. It walked and hunted on two legs.

WHAT'S IN A NAME?
Giganotosaurus means "giant lizard of the south."

DEFINITION
Two-legged dinosaurs are called theropods. Theropod means "beast foot." Theropods walked like birds.

ROUND 1

GIGANOTOSAURUS VS. STEGOSAURUS

MATCH 5

This dinosaur is easy to recognize. It had plates on its back and a spiked tail.

NAME FACT
Stegosaurus means "roof lizard."

MYSTERY
Did Stegosaurus have matching plates or alternating plates on its back?

It is no fun fighting Stegosaurus's plates and spiked tail, but Giganotosaurus's powerful jaw overpowers the slow Stegosaurus. After a vicious fight, Giganotosaurus wins.

GIGANOTOSAURUS WINS!

BRAIN FACT

Stegosaurus had the smallest brain-compared-to-body-size of any dinosaur. Its brain was only the size of a walnut.

DON'T BE CONFUSED

A different dinosaur had a similar name: Gigantosaurus. It was a sauropod.

Tyrannotitan lived about 100 million years ago. In real life it would never have met a Tyrannosaurus rex, or T. rex, which lived at a later time. Because Tyrannotitan lived in an earlier age, its brain was probably not as developed as T. rex's.

NAME FACT
Tyrannotitan means "giant tyrant."

ROUND 1 MATCH 6

TYRANNOTITAN VS. TYRANNOSAURUS REX

JUST CALL ME T. REX

Everyone knows this creature. It's one of the most famous dinosaurs. "Go, T. rex, go!"

TIMELINE
T. rex lived about 65 million years ago.

T. rex is smarter. It runs at Tyrannotitan and bites off an arm. Tyrannotitan is shocked.

UNSOLVED

No one knows for sure why T. rex had two tiny arms and only two tiny fingers.

As it decides what to do next, T. rex charges full speed and bites a chunk out of its neck. The fight is over!

T. REX WINS!

Horns, horns everywhere! It would hurt to bite this dinosaur's face. Styracosaurus was an herbivore. Its teeth were perfect for slicing and munching plants.

DEFINITION
Herbivores eat only plants.

FACT
Little horns are called hornlets.

ROUND 1

STYRACOSAURUS VS. SPINOSAURUS

MATCH 7

"SPIKED LIZARD" VS. "SPINED LIZARD"

Behold Spinosaurus! It may have been the perfect fighting dinosaur. It was fast, strong, light, and long. It had huge teeth on its jaw, and it could swim.

COLOR FACT
No one really knows what color the dinosaurs were or if they were multicolored.

Many dinosaur fans are rooting for Spinosaurus to win the championship. Spinosaurus could hunt on land and in the water. Go, Spinosaurus, go!

Spinosaurus goes head-to-head with Styracosaurus. Ouch! Too many sharp horns! They hurt. Styracosaurus is too slow.

NAME FACT
Spinosaurus means "spine lizard."

MOUTH FACT
Styracosaurus's mouth was shaped like a beak.

Shifty Spinosaurus sneaks around to the back of Styracosaurus. Spinosaurus bites Styracosaurus in the rear end. Styracosaurus is bleeding. This fight is over! No surprise here. Speed beats horns.

SPINOSAURUS WINS!

Many Allosaurus fossils have been discovered around the world. One dig site alone in Utah produced 60 different Allosaurus specimens. This dinosaur ate meat and walked on two legs. Its vertebrae bones were shaped differently than other dinosaurs. We may never know if it hunted in packs or alone.

DEFINITION
Vertebrae are an animal's backbones.

NAME FACT
Allosaurus means "different lizard."

ROUND 1

ALLOSAURUS VS. APATOSAURUS

MATCH 8

Apatosaurus was a long sauropod-type dinosaur with a tail like a bullwhip. When this huge creature walked, it must have sounded like thunder.

TRICKY NAME
Apatosaurus means "deceptive lizard." It is sometimes confused with Brontosaurus, which means "thunder lizard."

Allosaurus runs, opens its mouth, and jumps on Apatosaurus. Apatosaurus is huge, between 75-85 feet long. Apatosaurus can defend itself well. It waits for Allosaurus to make another charge. It turns its body, sets its four legs, and whips its tail. *Whack!*

FACT
Dinosaur footprints are also called trackways.

The tail hits Allosaurus across the neck and knocks the wind out of it. Another tail shot! *Whoosh! Whack!* That tail is huge! Allosaurus's neck is broken.

APATOSAURUS WINS!

Apatosaurus is the victor despite its small head and small brain.

On we go to the second round! Only eight dinosaurs are left. Kentrosaurus was armored with sharp weapons. It looked like it could inflict pain if attacked. Kentrosaurus did not look cute and huggable at all.

NAME FACT
A scientist that studies fossils and prehistoric life is called a paleontologist.

ROUND 2

KENTROSAURUS VS. ANKYLOSAURUS

MATCH 1

Ankylosaurus was defensively armored and plated for protection. Its body was low to the ground and difficult to attack. It looked like a tank. It even had horns covering its neck.

FACT
Ankylosaurus was twice as big as Kentrosaurus.

Both of these dinosaurs were herbivores. These two don't eat each other, so why would they fight? They might battle over territory, plants to eat, or water to drink.

The smaller Kentrosaurus hits Ankylosaurus with its tail. Its tail bounces off Ankylosaurus's armor. Ankylosaurus gets close, swings its hammer-like tail, and breaks Kentrosaurus's leg bones. *Whack! Whack!* Kentrosaurus falls over.

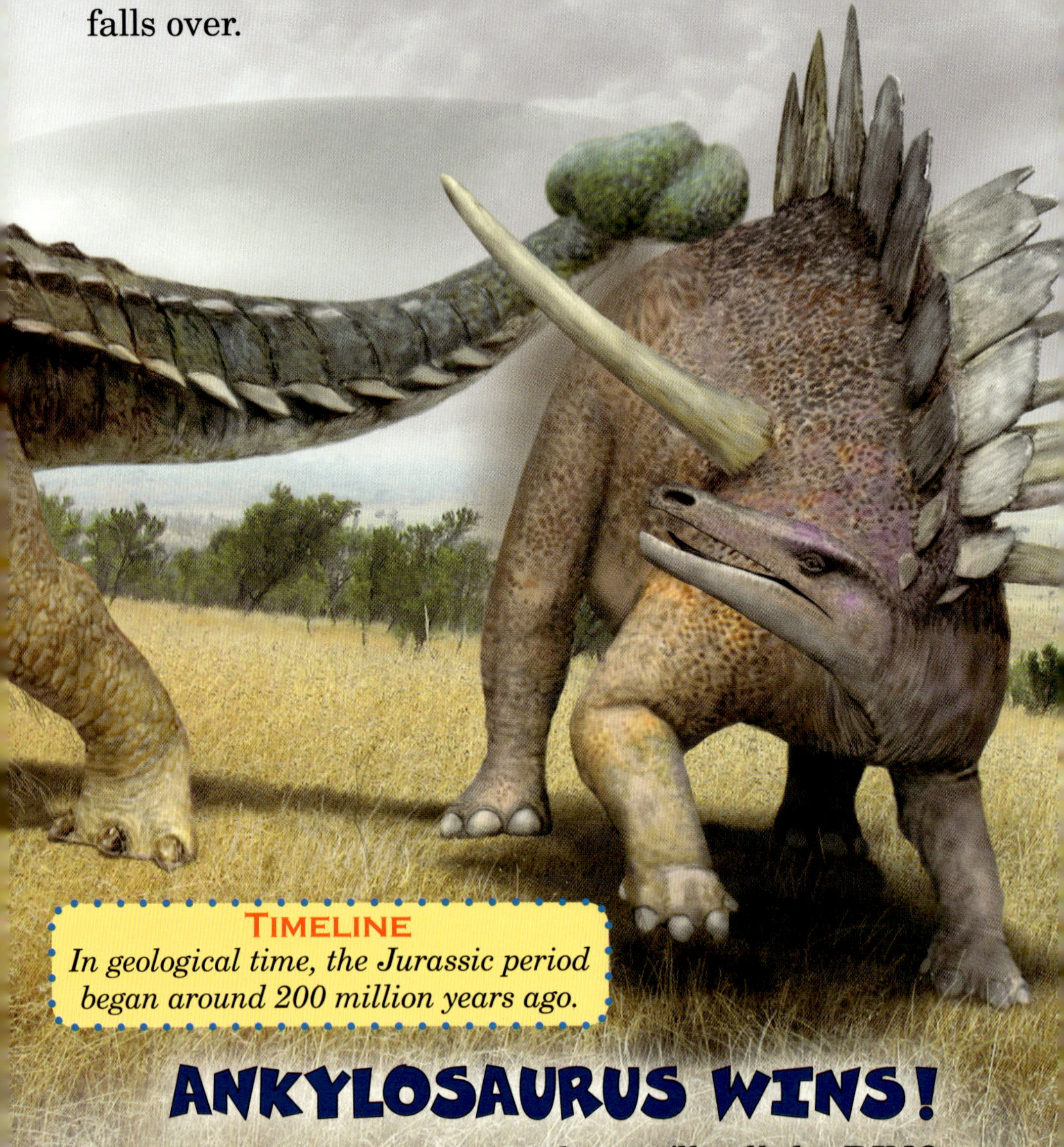

TIMELINE

In geological time, the Jurassic period began around 200 million years ago.

ANKYLOSAURUS WINS!

Ankylosaurus moves on to what we'll call the DINO FINAL FOUR.

This is a fight that fans have been waiting for. Giganotosaurus was bigger than T. rex. They both had a similar body design. Giganotosaurus had a huge jaw and strong legs.

FACT

Giganotosaurus had three fingers on each short arm.

ROUND 2 GIGANOTOSAURUS VS. TYRANNOSAURUS REX MATCH 2

T. rex had an advantage. Its jaw was much more powerful. Maybe T. rex was like an orca, also called a killer whale — a perfect hunting machine.

FOOT FACT

T. rex had four toes, just like a chicken. Three in front, one in back.

Giganotosaurus walks over to T. rex. It's not used to fightin an equal. T. rex pretends to bite but swings its body and whips Giganotosaurus with its heavy tail. T. rex attacks an gives Giganotosaurus something it didn't expect — a hip-check! While Giganotosaurus is off balance, T rex bites Giganotosaurus's neck. T. rex doesn't let go!

TYRANNOSAURUS REX WINS!

Once again we have a meat-eater against a plant-eater. We also could describe this fight as:

- *carnivore vs. herbivore*
- *enormous mouth vs. small mouth*
- *two legs vs. four legs*
- *hunter vs. forager*

DEFINITION
An animal forager searches for plants and other foods to eat.

DID YOU KNOW?
Yangchuanosaurus weighed about three tons.

ROUND 2 YANGCHUANOSAURUS VS. SUPERSAURUS MATCH 3

Supersaurus was one of the largest animals that ever walked on land. It weighed up to 40 tons. Its tail was up to 40 feet long. Its neck was longer than its tail.

OTHER HUGE SAUROPODS
Ultrasaurus, Giganotosaurus, Brachiosaurus, Argentinosaurus, or Diplodocus could have been in this book. How could they fight an aggressive, sharp-toothed meat-eater? Their size and height were great advantages.

As Yangchuanosaurus leaps and tries to bite chunks out of its foe, Supersaurus just trots toward Yangchuanosaurus and gets ready to step on it. Forty tons is a lot of weight. Supersaurus's body is high in the air, hard for Yangchuanosaurus to reach. Supersaurus bumps the smaller dinosaur with its long neck, then rises up on its hind legs and crushes Yangchuanosaurus with its feet.

TIMELINE
The Triassic period began around 250 million years ago.

Yangchuanosaurus has broken ribs and a broken leg. Good-bye, Yangchuanosaurus!

SUPERSAURUS WINS!

Supersaurus is the third dinosaur to get to the DINO FINAL FOUR.

Apatosaurus was a huge dinosaur. It ate up to 800 pounds of vegetation per day. It was up to 75 feet long. Scientists say it kept on growing and growing.

ROUND 2

APATOSAURUS VS. SPINOSAURUS

MATCH 4

DID YOU KNOW?
Spinosaurus may have fought ancient crocodiles.

Spinosaurus can send shivers down your spine. It is fast, long, and has a strong jaw with scary teeth. It is bigger than a T. rex but first it must defeat Apatosaurus.

Spinosaurus walks near Apatosaurus but stays out of range of its swinging head and whiplike tail. When Apatosaurus turns its head, Spinosaurus jumps up and rips a chunk out of its shoulder. Apatosaurus's shoulder starts bleeding. Spinosaurus runs to the other side and bites again.

SPINOSAURUS WINS!

Championship match coming soon!

DINO FINAL FOUR

This rugged plant-eater can smell the T. rex. It knows the T. rex is a troublemaker.

ARMOR FACT

Ankylosaurus's armor was on top. Not much was on its underbelly.

ROUND 3 — ANKYLOSAURUS VS. TYRANNOSAURUS REX — MATCH 1

When it was younger, T. rex got whacked by an Ankylosaurus tail. It hasn't forgotten the painful bump it got on its head.

T. rex runs full speed with its head down. *Smash!* T. rex knows the Ankylosaurus's armor is too thick to bite. T. rex needs to flip it over so it can bite its softer belly. Ankylosaurus is now helpless on its back.

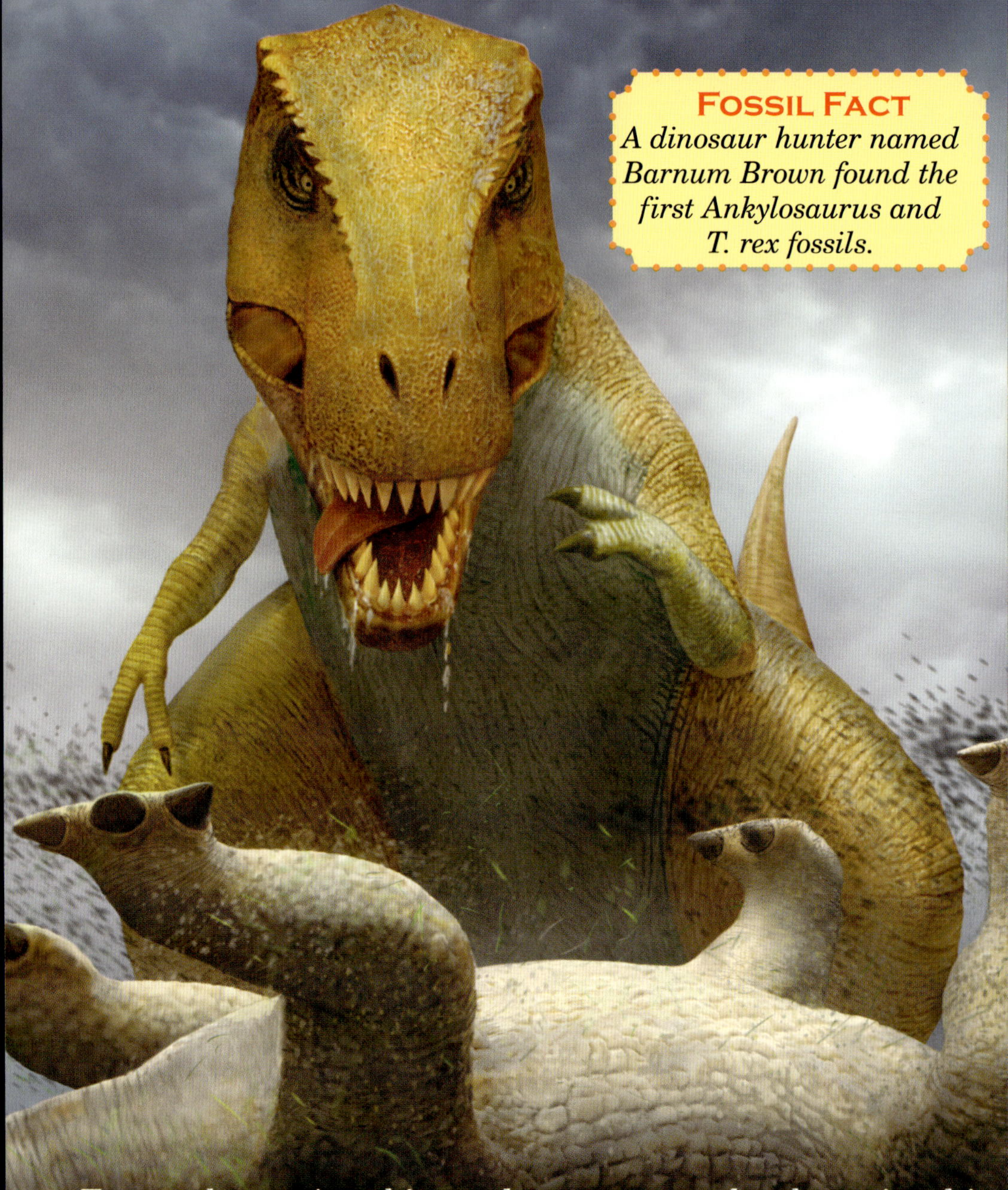

FOSSIL FACT

A dinosaur hunter named Barnum Brown found the first Ankylosaurus and T. rex fossils.

T. rex takes a giant bite and moves on to the championship match.

T. REX WINS!

It sounds like thunder as Supersaurus approaches Spinosaurus. *Boom! Boom! Boom!* go its feet.

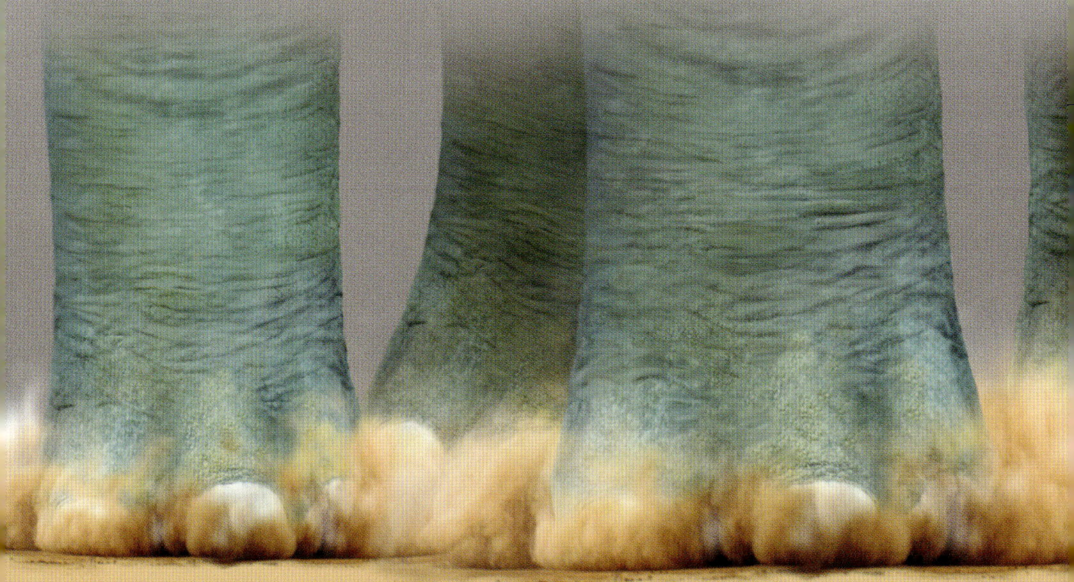

ROUND 3

SUPERSAURUS VS. SPINOSAURUS

MATCH 2

QUESTION?
Would the versatile Spinosaurus prefer to fight on land, in a swamp, or in deep water?

DEFINITION
Versatile means able to adapt to different situations.

Spinosaurus is fast. It runs at Supersaurus and attacks it between its front and back legs.

Spinosaurus has plenty of energy. It bites and backs off, the bites and backs off again. Spinosaurus avoids Supersaurus' huge tail and long neck. It takes time, but Supersaurus lose too much blood and eventually collapses.

SPINOSAURUS WINS!

On to the finals!

CHAMPIONSHIP MATCH!

TYRANNOSAURUS REX VS. SPINOSAURUS

The long-necks are gone! The armored dinosaurs are gone! The plant-eaters are gone! The spiked dinosaurs are gone! The plated dinosaurs are gone!

This is the fight that readers and dinosaurs have been waiting for — Jaw vs. Jaw!

T. rex has a stronger and wider jaw. Spinosaurus is longer but thinner. Spinosaurus also has a longer jaw. Both dinosaurs have a mouth full of sharp teeth. T. rex charges, but quicker Spinosaurus jumps out of the way.

Spinosaurus runs headfirst and bites T. rex's jaw. Spinosaurus's biting muscles are way stronger than the muscles T. rex uses to open its mouth.

Spinosaurus bites harder and deeper. Now T. rex can't bite back. Spinosaurus holds on. It uses its longer arms to scratch T. rex. T. rex loses.

SPINOSAURUS WINS!

This is one way the competition might have ended. Write your own ending or think of a new version of an Ultimate Rumble book.